Westward Expansion

AMERICA'S PUSH TO THE PACIFIC

THE ERIE CANAL

JEANNE NAGLE

Britannica Educational Publishing

IN ASSOCIATION WITH

ROSEN EDUCATIONAL SERVICES

Published in 2018 by Britannica Educational Publishing (a trademark of Encyclopædia Britannica, Inc.) in association with The Rosen Publishing Group, Inc.
29 East 21st Street, New York, NY 10010

Distributed exclusively by Rosen Publishing.
To see additional Britannica Educational Publishing titles, go to rosenpublishing.com.

First Edition

Britannica Educational Publishing
J.E. Luebering: Executive Director, Core Editorial
Andrea R. Field: Managing Editor, Compton's by Britannica

Rosen Publishing
Heather Moore Niver: Editor
Nelson Sá: Art Director
Tahara Anderson: Designer
Cindy Reiman: Photography Manager
Heather Moore Niver: Photo Researcher

Library of Congress Cataloging-in-Publication Data

Names: Nagle, Jeanne, author.
Title: The Erie Canal / Jeanne Nagle.
Description: New York : Britannica Educational Publishing, in Association with Rosen Educational Services, 2018. | Series: Westward expansion: America's push to the Pacific | Includes bibliographical references and index. | Audience: Grades 5–8.
Identifiers: LCCN 2017014856| ISBN 9781680487879 (library bound) | ISBN 9781680487862 (pbk.) | ISBN 9781538300121 (6 pack)
Subjects: LCSH: Erie Canal (N.Y.)—History—Juvenile literature.
Classification: LCC HE396.E6 N364 2018 | DDC 386/.4809747—dc23
LC record available at https://lccn.loc.gov/2017014856

Manufactured in the United States of America

Photo credits: Cover, p. 25 Bettmann/Getty Images; p. 5 Encyclopædia Britannica, Inc.; p. 8 Culture Club/Hulton Archives/Getty Images; p. 10 From The New York Public Library/510d47da-2264-a3d9-e040-e00a18064a99; p. 13 Universal Images Group/Getty Images; p. 14 Hulton Archive/Archive Photos/Getty Images; p. 15 Smith Collection/Gado/Archive Photos/Getty Images; p. 17 From The New York Public Library/510d47e1-4d74-a3d9-e040-e00a18064a99; p. 20 Private Collection/© Look and Learn/Bridgeman Images; p. 21 Daniel Borzynski/Alamy Stock Photo; p. 22 Hulton Archive/Getty Images; pp. 23, 30–31 Historical/Corbis Historical/Getty Images; p. 27 Underwood Archives/Archive Photos/Getty Images; p. 29 SuperStock/Getty Images; p. 32 The New York Historical Society/Archive Photos/Getty Images; pp. 34–35 The New York Historical Society/Hulton Fine Art Collection/Getty Images; p. 36 nsf/Alamy Stock Photo; p. 37 Chicago History Museum/Archive Photos/Getty Images; p. 40 Fotosearch/Archive Photos/Getty Images; p. 41 George Ostertag/Alamy Stock Photo; cover and interior pages (banner) Library of Congress Prints and Photographs Division.

CONTENTS

INTRODUCTION

The American frontier was an escape and a place of hope for those willing and able to take their futures into their own hands. Celebrated then and ever since in poetry, short stories, novels, drama, films, music, and paintings, the epic westward movement in the United States has never failed to excite the imaginations of people everywhere.

In the United States, the frontier moved in stages, beginning with the eastern settlements, the original thirteen colonies. After the American Revolution, the pioneers gradually crossed the Appalachian Mountains and went into the Ohio and Mississippi river valleys.

Some settlers arrived with eyes open and were happy with what they found. Many did not expect the real frontier, which was a hard place to live in. Most of the normal expectations of life were missing. One made do with what was available, and normally that was very little. Grinding poverty was the living standard, at least until the frontier began to give way to civilization.

As the country expanded westward, settlers in western New York, Pennsylvania, and Ohio were faced with the problem of transporting goods. The places to sell their farm products were the large eastern cities, such as New York City. In turn, the settlers needed the supplies and manufactured goods that were sold in these cities. Wagon freight was too expensive—it cost a hundred dollars to send one ton of freight from Buffalo to New York City, and the trip took twenty days. The new flat-bottomed river steamships offered cheap transportation, but there were no through water routes between the large population centers of the East and the farmlands of the developing West.

Canals, built to link natural waterways, were the solution. The Erie Canal was the first canal in the United States to connect the Great Lakes with the Atlantic Ocean.

Map of the Erie Canal.

The 363-mile (584-kilometer) canal was constructed from 1817 to 1825 along the Mohawk River, between the Hudson River and Lake Erie. It connected Lake Erie at the city of Buffalo in the western part of the state with Albany, the state capital located in the east. At Albany, the canal met with the Hudson River, which runs south to New York City and empties into New York Bay at the southern tip of Manhattan Island.

The success of the Erie Canal propelled New York City into becoming a major commercial center and encouraged canal construction throughout the United States. With ready access to markets, settlers moved into upstate New York and western territories.

The importance of the canal to the early expansion of the United States cannot be overstated. It opened the Great Lakes region to industry and farming, and it provided a market for manufactured goods from the East. By creating the nation's first east–west water-trade link, the canal encouraged westward expansion.

CHAPTER ONE

WESTWARD HO!

In the middle of the 1700s, both Britain and France controlled land in North America. Britain controlled the thirteen colonies that later became the United States. Under French rule was the area called New France. It included large parts of what is now eastern Canada and also covered much of the Great Lakes region and areas west of the Appalachian Mountains.

Both countries wanted the upper Ohio River valley, in what is now northeastern Ohio and western Pennsylvania. The French built a chain of forts from the St. Lawrence River to the Mississippi and were trading with the Native Americans in the area. However, this land was claimed by Virginia under its "sea-to-sea" grant from England. People from the British colonies were starting settlements in what they called the western frontier.

The conflict over the Ohio River valley led to an epic struggle between the two countries—the French

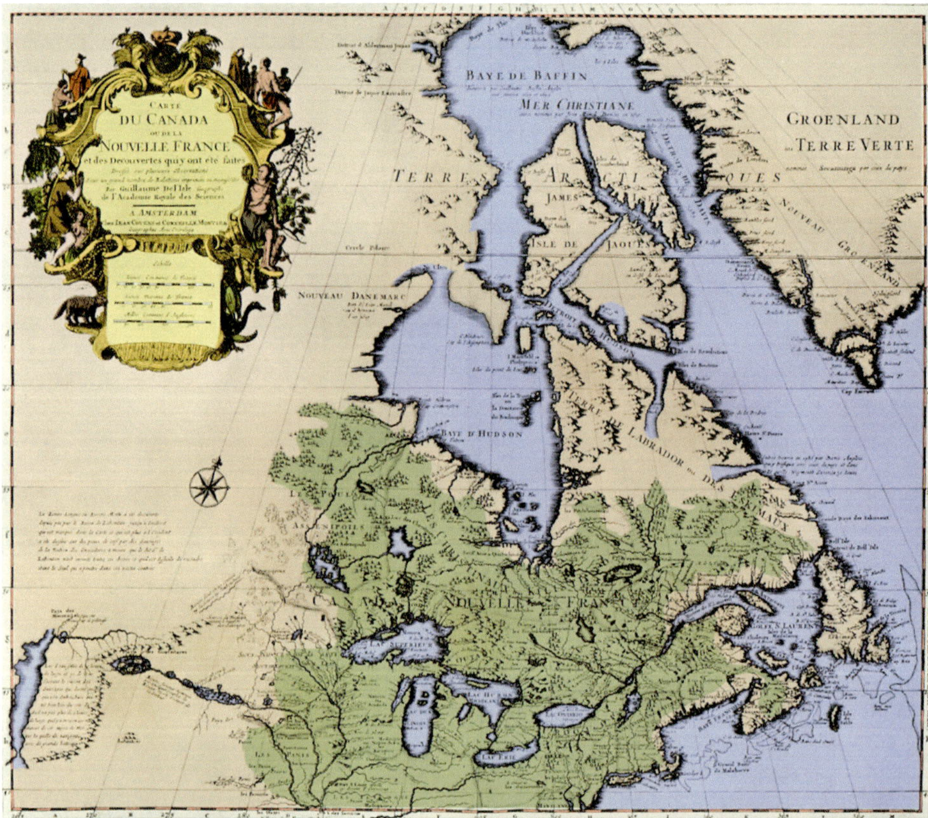

Map detailing land that constituted "New France," denoted in green, circa the early eighteenth century. The French were at odds with the British over disputed trade routes in the area.

and Indian War, which lasted from 1754 to 1763. By 1760 the British had captured all of New France. The war ended when Britain and France signed the Treaty of Paris on February 10, 1763.

After the American Revolution ended in 1783, this wilderness area became part of the United States of America. The Ordinance of 1787 provided that from three to five states could be carved from the territory's limits. After the land was surveyed, it was quickly occupied. The new country was expanding westward.

OPENING TRADE

Settling the western frontier was one thing. Making it a viable place to live, however, was another. Using what is known as subsistence farming, settlers in Ohio and farther west could certainly feed themselves from their own livestock and whatever crops they produced. Yet farmers and other tradesmen also needed a healthy market for what they grew, raised, or produced. Likewise, western settlers needed to purchase clothes, furniture, and other manufactured goods that came out of eastern cities.

Distance and a certain degree of isolation from the larger, established eastern cities and towns made trade difficult, to say the least. Hauling goods and people by land to what was known then as "the interior" of the United States took quite a while. The shortest distance between two points is a straight line, but there was no straight-through path from the East to the interior, thanks to the Appalachian mountain range. Getting around the Appalachians added time to the journey.

New York City, Philadelphia, and Baltimore were all rivals for the trade of the growing interior of the United States, namely the Ohio River valley and the western frontier. Location favored New York in the struggle. It could tap the lowest route through the Appalachians by way of the Mohawk River valley.

HARNESSING THE MOHAWK

Beginning in the 1780s, various plans were proposed to improve navigation on the Mohawk River. In 1792 the Western Inland Lock Navigation Company was

Print showing travelers on a bridged road that crossed the Mohawk River. The Mohawk was the site of early canal construction in the United States.

incorporated by the state of New York and given the rights to improve navigation on rivers and lakes west of Albany. Under the leadership of Philip Schuyler, the company focused most of its activity on the Mohawk River, clearing the riverbed and digging several short canals to bypass river rapids. Although the company achieved some success in making improvements to the river, it never had the financial resources to tackle the larger navigation obstacles in the river.

The Western Inland Lock Navigation Company, which found itself short of funds and snarled in state partisan politics, never completed its plans. Nonetheless, the Mohawk River still provided a valuable path from the Atlantic Ocean to the Great Lakes, and plans for a new canal were debated. In 1820 the state purchased the company's works, closing the books on the eighteenth-century canal plans. Meanwhile, a new canal project had been gaining momentum in New York State.

SELECTING THE ROUTE

As early as 1808, Albert Gallatin, then secretary of the treasury, made a survey of all available transportation routes in the United States. As a result of this survey, he recommended the building of a great many canals. One of the canals he proposed was

General, President, Canal Builder

Canals were a great help in developing transportation and commerce in the United States. Revolutionary War hero and future United States president George Washington was among the first statesmen to realize how important they might be. He headed the Potomac Company, which was formed to improve navigation along Virginia's Potomac River. The company's plan was to build a trench, with a system of locks, alongside the river's length—in other words, to construct a canal.

The Chesapeake and Ohio Canal, as the project became known, was not completed until 1850. However, several shorter canals connecting rivers were built in the early days of the United States. The first was dug at South Hadley, Massachusetts, between 1792 and 1796.

meant to link the Hudson River in New York with the Great Lakes in the western territory.

The proposed canals were much longer than any that had previously been dug in the United States. In addition, the costs and the engineering problems were so great that most people regarded Gallatin's proposals as impractical. DeWitt Clinton, then the powerful mayor of New York City, thought otherwise. Although originally he had supported a Hudson–Great Lakes link for reasons of political expediency, Clinton soon became convinced of the canal's importance to the economic future of his state.

Reproduction of a painting by artist Alonzo Chappel depicting US secretary of the treasury Albert Gallatin, whose transportation survey led to the construction of the Erie Canal.

Another New York state politician also was interested in canal building. While serving in the state assembly, lawyer and civil engineer James Geddes met the New York surveyor general, Simeon De Witt, who persuaded him that a canal connecting the Hudson River and the Great Lakes was feasible. Geddes then traveled around the state to gather information and to arouse enthusiasm; despite his lack of technical training, he surveyed a possible route in 1808 and reported his findings to the assembly on January 20, 1809.

In 1811, DeWitt Clinton proposed a bill in the New York state senate to appoint a commission to explore routes for a canal across the state. The goal was to link coastal trade from the Northeast with the Great Lakes via

Engraving of then-New York state legislator DeWitt Clinton, the mastermind of, and driving force behind, construction of the Erie Canal.

Lake Erie. De Witt himself, along with six other members of the commission, set out to survey the proposed canal path in July of that year. The path chosen was very similar to the one proposed by Geddes.

STOPPING AND STARTING ANEW

Plans for the canal and, indeed, all work of the commission were put on hold beginning in 1812, when the United States entered into war once again with Great Britain. The War of 1812 lasted two years; when it ended, the canal idea was revived. Clinton and statesman Gouverneur Morris, who was chairman of the canal commission, unsuccessfully sought federal aid for the project in Washington, DC. Subsequently, the group went to the state capital at Albany, urging acceptance of a detailed plan. De Witt won preliminary legislative approval in 1816 and was named commissioner for the project.

Portrait of canal commission chairman Gouverneur Morris, who petitioned the US federal government for funds to reinvigorate the stalled canal project in New York State.

The following year, Clinton was elected governor of New York, a position he held for two terms. As governor, he persuaded the state legislature to authorize loans for $7 million to build a canal from Buffalo to the upper Hudson. In honor of the western connection point at Lake Erie, it would be called the Erie Canal.

CHAPTER TWO

DIGGING IN: BUILDING THE CANAL

Canals serve a number of different purposes. They may be dug to drain low areas, float away sewage, bring water to dry farmlands, or carry water from storage in reservoirs to city water-supply systems. Some are built as "detours" in rivers, allowing boats to avoid waterfalls, rapid, and dams. In the modern era, some canals provide a swift flow of water to make electricity at hydroelectric plants. The most important are the navigation canals that connect or take the place of natural bodies of water. Such is the case with the Erie Canal.

GETTING STARTED

The Erie Canal was designed to connect Lake Erie at Buffalo, New York, with the Hudson River at the cities of Troy and Albany, for a water distance of 363 miles

Stereograph card depicting the mouth of the Erie Canal at Buffalo, New York, in the 1800s. The city is on the eastern tip of Lake Erie, the body of water from which the canal took its name.

(584 km). With a typical canal prism shape—40 feet (12 meters) across on the top, 28 feet (8.5 m) wide at the bottom, and 4 feet (1.2 m) deep—it was patterned after the Middlesex Canal in Massachusetts, which opened at 1804. Canals in England also served as useful models.

The plan was to start near the middle of the canal's length and dig in both directions, east and west, at the same time. As digging began, the project was divided into three parts. The western segment of the canal ran from Lake Erie to Montezuma, outside of Rochester; the middle stretched from Montezuma to Utica; and the eastern portion extended from Utica to Albany, where the canal would meet the Hudson River.

Construction began on July 4, 1817, near Rome, New York. Essentially at the canal's middle, the location was selected as the project's starting point because surveys indicated that workers would encounter fewer natural obstacles there than they would in the western or eastern segments. Work was undertaken by multiple contractors who agreed to dig small sections of the canal. Each contractor was responsible for supplying equipment and for hiring, supervising, and paying his own workers.

Benjamin Wright

Benjamin Wright directed the construction of the Erie Canal. Trained as a surveyor in his youth, Wright was working as surveyor near Rome, New York, when he was hired by the New York State Canal Commission. As chief engineer, Wright himself directed work on the canal's middle division, between Rome and Waterford. He also was in charge of overseeing work on the especially difficult eastern division of the canal.

Wright resigned from the Erie Canal project in 1827, later serving as chief engineer on other canal projects throughout the state. He also made land surveys for railroads in New York, Illinois, and Cuba. Because he trained so many engineers on the Erie Canal project, at a time when there was no formal training in engineering in the United States, Wright has been called the "father of American engineering."

THE CREW

The contractors, or crew chiefs, who were chosen to oversee each small portion of canal construction often were residents of the towns and cities surrounding the emerging waterway. The Erie Canal Commission figured, rightly so, that men who already had a stake in the land would be invested in making the canal a success and would work hard to make that happen. Many of the first workers that the contractors hired also were local. Soon laborers from New England joined the local workforce, including plenty of farmhands who were happy to temporarily switch jobs if it meant a bigger paycheck. Because the work was backbreaking and could be dangerous, crew members were paid well for their time and effort. Later, they would be joined by immigrants who traveled to America to earn wages that were much higher than they could make at home. The Irish were heavily represented among the immigrant workers; Germans also were part of the crew.

TOOLS OLD AND NEW

Using horses and manpower, the canal was dug across New York State. Mechanized construction equipment, such as backhoes and steam shovels, had not yet been invented. Workers used shovels, pickaxes, and other

Schoolbook illustration showing canal diggers at work on the Erie Canal, under the watchful eye of an engineer (left, pointing) who oversaw the building.

manual tools to dig the canal trench. Some clever workmen attached the flat end of a blade horizontally to a plow, creating a kind of mini-bulldozer that could cut small roots so that they could be more easily removed. When workers ran into layers of rock and stone, they used hand drills to create cradles for gunpowder, which was used to blast through the obstacles.

Workers employed a number of ingenious methods for overcoming construction obstacles. Canal engineer Canvass White solved a critical problem when he discovered how to create a cement that hardened underwater. Having a local source of this cement greatly aided the construction process, and it reduced costs by eliminating the need to import European cement.

Another time-saving invention involved the removal of trees that grew along the canal's path. One device allowed a single worker to pull trees up by their roots. A chain was attached to the top branches and then wound around a secured roller, operated by a crank. As the top of the tree was pulled toward the ground, the pressure caused the roots to pop up and out of the dirt.

When trees had to be cut down, workers took advantage of a special stump puller designed by canal workers. An axle was attached to two giant wheels that were kept from rolling by blocks. A rope tied around a third, smaller wheel in the middle of the axle was pulled by a team of oxen or horses, making the axle spin. One end of a heavy chain was attached to the spinning axle, and the other was secured around the stump. Tension and motion quickly removed the tree remains, roots and all.

LOCKS AND AQUEDUCTS

Photo of an abandoned lock once in service on the Miami and Erie Canal in Ohio. Canal locks ensure that water levels rise or fall, depending on the need.

When two natural bodies of water stand at different levels, building a canal between them presents a complicated engineering problem. To make up for the difference in level, engineers build

How Canal Locks Work

Canal locks are long, rectangular artificial water basins with concrete walls and a pair of gates at each end. When a vessel is traveling upstream, the upper gates stay closed as the ship enters the lock at the lower water level. The downstream gates are then closed, and more water is pumped into the basin. The rising water lifts the vessel to the level of the upper body of water. The upper gates then open, and the boat passes through. The opposite occurs for downstream travel. The ship enters the lock from the upper level, and water is pumped from the lock until the ship is in line with the lower level.

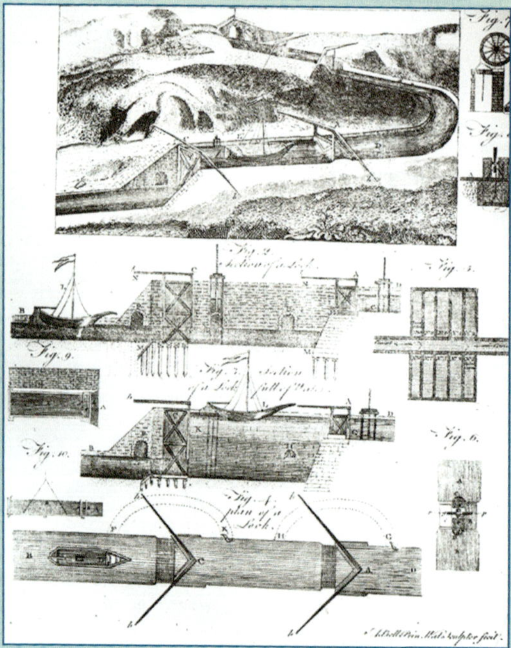

These engineering diagrams, dated from around the late 1700s, detail the design as well as the function of canal locks.

one or more water "steps," called locks, that carry boats up or down between the two levels. In order to move boats through more than 500 feet (152 m) of elevation,

Artist's rendering of the Rochester, New York, aqueduct. The structure allowed the waters of the Erie Canal to cross the Genesee River, which provided the growing city with water power.

the Erie Canal required eighty-three locks, each made of stone and spaced at intervals along the length of the waterway. The locks were designed so that each needed only one person for its operation.

The canal also required the construction of eighteen aqueducts to carry the canal over natural bodies of water. With its locks and aqueducts, the canal was considered an American engineering marvel.

CHAPTER THREE

GETTING RESULTS

A few years into construction of the canal, things weren't going as well as the commission had hoped. Delays were caused by difficulties with the tricky eastern and western segments, and it looked as if the proposed completion date was going to be greatly delayed. Subsequently, DeWitt Clinton came under political attack, and his pet project was mockingly called "Clinton's Ditch." People thought that the canal would never be finished and that the money New York State had allotted for construction was going to be wasted.

They were wrong, on both counts. Canal construction was completed on October 25, 1825, two years ahead of the revised schedule. In a grand ceremony, Clinton and other dignitaries boarded the *Seneca Chief* in Buffalo and traveled the length of the canal. At the conclusion of the trip in New York City, Clinton emptied a keg of water from Lake Erie into the Atlantic Ocean, calling it the "marriage of the waters."

Governor DeWitt Clinton empties a keg of water from Lake Erie into the Atlantic Ocean at New York City during a ceremony to mark the opening of the Erie Canal.

In the end, the canal had cost more than the planned $7 million to build, but it earned back this sum in the first ten years of operation. The Erie Canal would prove to be a great source of pride and an example of how citizens could band together to improve upon nature and promote progress.

QUICKER AND CHEAPER

The canal was an instant commercial and financial success. "Clinton's Ditch" soon bustled with freight and passenger traffic. Flat-bottomed barges carried cargo from Buffalo to New York City, as well as to several canal towns in between. Passenger-only boats were known as packets. Line boats usually had space for both people and freight. Tolls were collected from all that passed through the canal. Historian Peter Bernstein notes that revenue from the canal's first year of operation was more than $500,000.

Trade moved in both directions as manufactured goods from eastern cities were carried on the canal into western towns and villages. Pulled by mules or horses that walked along the water on towpaths, canal boats were capable of carrying thirty tons of produce—far more than wagons could—which greatly lowered the cost of transporting products. Prices to carry grain from

Painting of a packet boat on the canal, circa 1840. Imagine the man on the right warning passengers they would have to duck soon by yelling "Low bridge, everybody down!"

the Midwest to New York began to fall. In 1836 a million bushels of western grain were unloaded in Buffalo; by 1840 the load was four million. Transshipped to canal boats, the grain was sent to towns such as Rochester or New York City, where it was processed into flour.

The time it took to conduct trade also was drastically reduced. Goods could be shipped between New York City and the Great Lakes region in eight days, at a

A Site to Behold

The Erie Canal turned out to be more than a way to transport goods to and from America's interior. From the moment it opened, the canal was also a tourist attraction. As the longest continuous canal in the world at that time, and an engineering marvel, people came from miles around—even from Europe—just to take a ride on one or more of its segments. They could sleep on packet boats, but the accommodations were crowded and uncomfortable. There also was the option to disembark and stay at one of the inns that had opened up in canal towns.

Some tourists combined their Erie Canal voyage with a side trip to a nearby natural wonder, Niagara Falls. The falls could be reached by traveling up the Niagara River from the canal town of Tonawanda, near Buffalo. Others elected to shop and see the sites in New York City.

fraction of the old cost. Relay teams of horses or mules pulled light passenger packet boats through the canal from Buffalo to Albany in three and a half days.

In just nine years, tolls charged on the canal, for passengers and freight, had completely repaid the state loan. Tolls were then put into the Canal Fund, through which the commission was able to finance several branch canals in the state.

Horses on a towpath pull a packet boat along the Erie Canal while a raft passes, powered by a pole.

POPULATION SHIFT

After the American Revolution, a flood of people crossed the mountains into the fertile lands between the Appalachians and the Mississippi River. By 1810, Ohio, Tennessee, and Kentucky had been transformed from wilderness into a region of farms and towns.

Despite those decades of continuous westward pushing of the frontier line, it was not until the conclusion of the War of 1812 that the westward movement grew into a significant outpouring of people across the continent.

The westward movement after the War of 1812 at first left the Great Lakes untouched. Transportation was so difficult that few settlers found their way into the lake regions. But the opening of the Erie Canal in 1825 brought a stream of immigration. With ready access to markets, settlers moved into upstate New York and western territories. Many farmers abandoned their land in New England in favor of the rich farmland to be had in what would become known as the American Midwest.

STRENGTHENING THE STATE

Towns along the waterway's route developed lively trade based on canal traffic. The Erie Canal helped Rochester's rapid growth, and by the 1840s it had become a prosperous flour-milling town. The canal also increased the flow of traffic through Albany, which

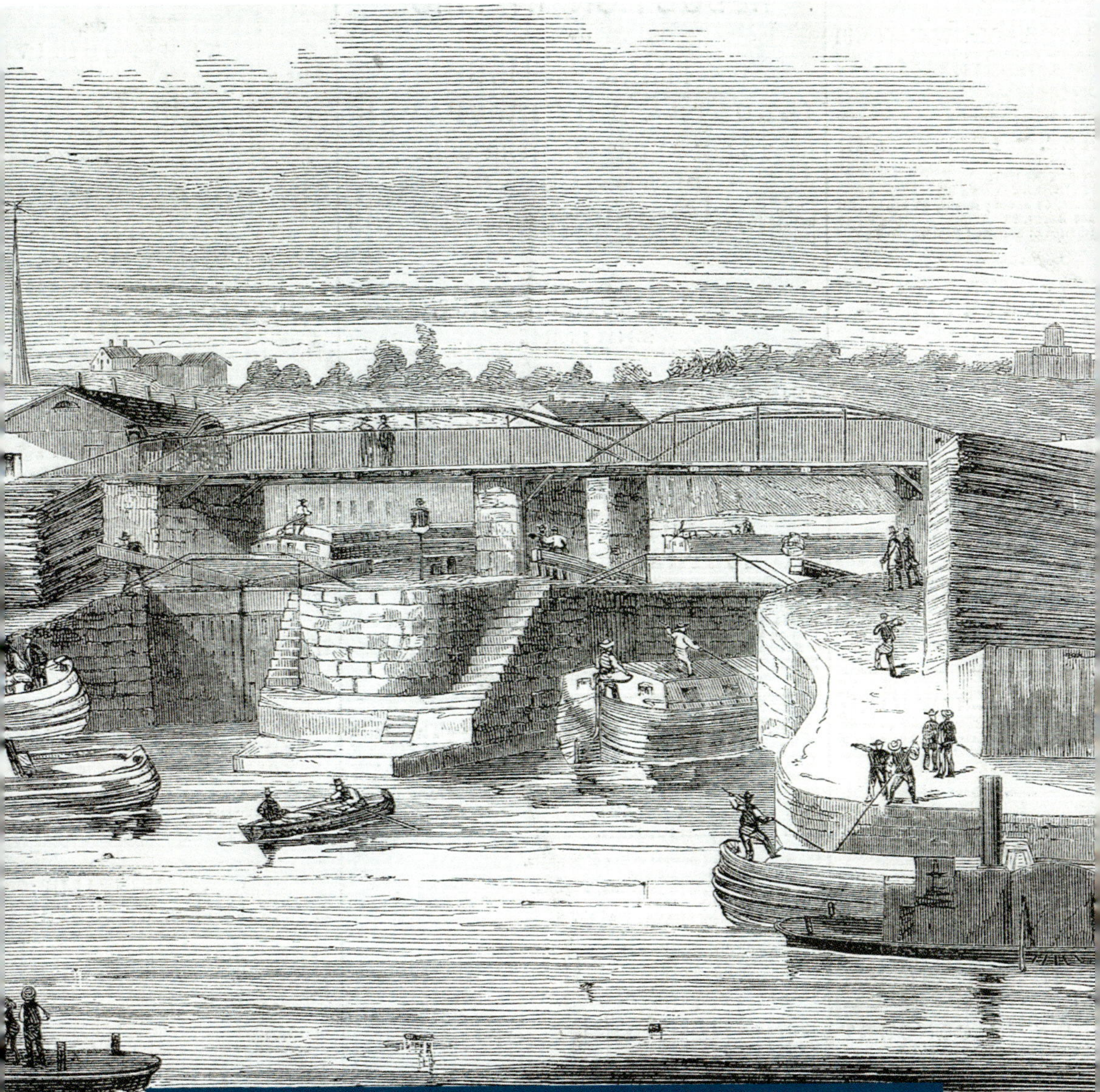

Where the Hudson River met the canal stood Albany, which became an important stop for people and merchandise moving westward after traveling north from New York City ports.

ANCE OF THE ERIE CANAL FROM THE HUDSON RIVER, AT ALBANY, N. Y.

A box that held a medal commemorating the opening of the Erie Canal, presented by the city of New York—which benefited greatly from the existence of the waterway.

became the hub of transportation to Michigan Territory (the upper Great Lakes). Buffalo became a major transportation port as farm produce from Ohio, Indiana, Illinois, Michigan, and Canada flowed through the city on its way to New York City.

The transformation of New York City into the country's center of trade was spurred in large part by the Erie Canal. By the mid-1800s the city handled more goods and people than all the other US ports combined. By 1900 it was the busiest port and one of the wealthiest cities in the world. The city also grew to be a major banking center after the Erie Canal opened.

CHAPTER FOUR

THE FATE OF THE CANAL

The canal did more than just move people to different locations and increase populations. Its arrival affected the entire nation by refocusing the economies of the Northeast states—particularly New York—from agriculture to industry. For the first two decades after the 1825 opening, canal communities experienced tremendous population growth, with the majority of people residing in and around larger cities. Steadily, these cities turned to production and manufacturing, rather than farming, to sustain themselves. Furthermore, the overwhelming success of the Erie Canal strengthened the resolve of those who believed canals were the transportation wave of the future, spurring a canal-building boom in North America.

SERVING AS INSPIRATION

At the start of the 19th century, only 100 miles (161 km) of canals had been built in the United States. Before

Painting by artist Walter M. Oddie showing a stretch of the Erie Canal seemingly far from the cities and busy ports along the canal's path.

the end of the century, more than 4,000 miles (6,437 km) of canals were open to navigation.

In 1830 the Ohio-Erie Canal connected the Ohio River, and thereby the Mississippi, to the Great Lakes and through them, the eastern seaboard cities. This made Cleveland an important shipping center, and it became incorporated as a city in 1836. As the northern terminus of the Ohio-Erie Canal, the city experienced a fourfold population increase in ten years.

To provide a southern route around the Allegheny Mountains, the Susquehanna and Ohio rivers were linked in 1834 by a 394-mile (634-km) canal between Philadelphia and Pittsburgh. A unique feature of this route was the combination of water and rail transport with a 37-mile (60-km) portage by rail via five inclined planes rising almost 1,400 feet (427 m) above sea level and then

A former lock of the Ohio-Erie Canal. Once a well-traveled waterway that bolstered parts of the Ohio territory, the canal was largely abandoned less than a century after it had opened.

falling 1,150 feet (351 m) to Johnstown on the far side of the mountains, where a 105-mile (169-km) canal with sixty-eight locks ran to Pittsburgh. Travel by this route was slow and expensive, and traffic was never very heavy. By 1856 a series of canals linked this canal system to the Erie Canal.

Meanwhile, the Louisiana Purchase of 1803 had given the United States control of the Mississippi River, which would become the main waterway for the movement of midwestern produce via New Orleans and the Gulf of

Illustration showing activity along the Illinois-Michigan Canal shortly after opening. This canal expanded the economic development of the United States westward to the Mississippi River and south to the Gulf of Mexico.

Mexico. A key development from this was the Illinois-Michigan Canal. Completed in 1848, the canal connected the two great water systems of the continent, the Great Lakes and the Mississippi River. Entering Lake Michigan at Chicago, then a mere village, the canal triggered the city's explosive growth. Later still, several canals were constructed subsequently to link up with the Erie Canal, Canada's Welland Canal, and the St. Lawrence River. Overall, the canal developments of the period established a comprehensive network of inland waterways.

THE CIVIL WAR CONNECTION

Early supporters of the Erie Canal claimed that it could help strengthen the country by tying the fortunes of the eastern states to the expanding western territories. Little did they know that this theory would be put to the test during the American Civil War.

The South depended on slaves to keep their economy going, so the Southern states were pro-slavery. The Northern states were abolitionist, meaning they were against slavery. There was a major disagreement regarding whether newly formed western states should be slaveholders. Because Northerners had such an easy route to the interior via the Erie Canal, many settlers in the western states came from the North and therefore held the same abolitionist views as other Northerners.

When the South seceded from the Union, the majority of western states sided with the North. Twenty-three Northern and western states that supported the federal government were pitted against eleven Southern states that had seceded. Historians believe that the greater number of states fighting for the Union was one factor in the North winning the war.

PACKET VERSUS BOXCAR

For decades the Erie Canal remained a popular method of shipment and passenger travel. Soon, however, the business of transporting freight and passengers along canal waterways faced stiff competition from America's railroads.

The first American railroads started from Atlantic ports, including Boston, Philadelphia, and New York City. Competition among the Atlantic ports meant that those with the poorest river connections to the West—Baltimore, Boston, and Charleston—became the earliest and strongest proponents of railroad promotion.

Within twenty years, four rail lines had crossed the Alleghenies to reach their goal on the "Western Waters" of the Great Lakes or on the tributaries of the Mississippi. Meanwhile other lines had started from west of the mountains; by the mid-1850s, Chicago, St. Louis, and Memphis were connected with the East. Still other lines were stretching westward beyond the Mississippi.

Competition between the Erie Canal and rail transportation was keen. Canal cities attracted the railroads, which built their tracks along a similar route taken by the canal. Fares were kept low for canal transportation in order to compete. However, trains made traveling and transporting goods easier and faster; furthermore, railways were cheaper and easier to build. After 1870, rail traffic in New York State surpassed canal traffic.

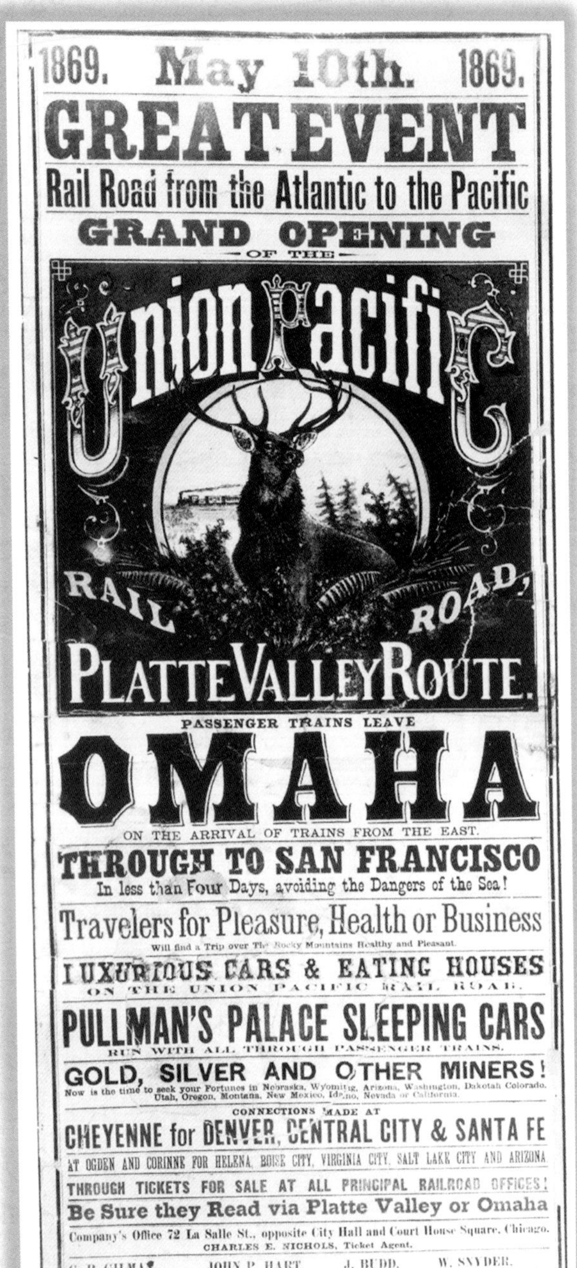

Poster for the Union Pacific Railroad, advertising transportation between Nebraska and California. Connections from eastern cities on other rail lines made coast-to-coast transportation by land quick and inexpensive.

ADAPTING AND ADJUSTING

The Erie Canal has been enlarged several times, the first time occurring in 1835.

In 1915 the whole canal system was overhauled, with the Erie Canal remaining a major link in what was called the New York State Barge Canal (later the New York State Canal System). This new waterway could handle larger steamships than before. In spite of this modernization, however, trade had changed. The

The Chittenango Landing Canal Boat Museum, outside Syracuse, New York. Museums and other landmarks help keep the history of the Erie Canal, and its importance to westward expansion, alive.

waterway could no longer compete against railroads or the new St. Lawrence Seaway, and traffic on the canal gradually dwindled.

As the chief link in the New York State Barge Canal system, the Erie Canal is still used to transport bulky products. Today, the New York State Canalway Trail uses more than 200 miles (322 km) of the Barge Canal, including segments of the original Erie Canal, for recreation purposes.

Yet the glory days of the Erie Canal live on in history. This symbol of American ingenuity and can-do spirit will always be remembered as a crucial element in the early days of the country's legendary westward expansion.

GLOSSARY

accommodations Lodging, food, and services or traveling space and related services.

aqueduct A structure for conveying a canal over a river or hollow.

barge A roomy usually flat-bottomed boat used chiefly for the transport of goods on inland waterways and usually propelled by towing.

contractor One who contracts to perform work or provide supplies.

dwindle To become steadily less, to shrink.

emerging Newly formed and prominent.

epic Extending beyond the usual or ordinary, especially in size or scope.

expansion Increasing the extent or scope of something.

feasible Capable of being done or carried out.

isolation The act of being set apart from others.

lock In a waterway, an enclosure with gates at each end used in raising or lowering boats as they pass from level to level.

momentum Strength or force gained by motion or by a series of events.

overhauled The state of being reexamined and redone or approved upon.

packet boat A canalboat designed to carry passengers.

subsistence A source or means of obtaining the necessities of life.

survey To examine as to condition, situation, or value.

tradesman A worker in an occupation requiring special manual or mechanical skill.

tributary A stream feeding a larger stream or a lake.

viable Capable of growing or developing.

FOR FURTHER READING

Aller, Susan Bivin. *What Difference Could a Waterway Make? And Other Questions About the Erie Canal.* Minneapolis, MN: Lerner Publishing Group, Inc., 2011.

Coleman, Wim, and Pat Perrin. *The Amazing Erie Canal and How a Big Ditch Opened Up the West.* New York, NY: Enslow Publishers, Inc., 2006.

Drake, Patricia. *New York's Erie Canal* (Spotlight on New York). New York, NY: PowerKids Press, 2014.

Kendall, Martha E. *The Erie Canal.* New York, NY: National Geographic Children's Books, 2008.

Kleinmartin, Hex. *The Erie Canal* (Expanding America). New York, NY: Cavendish Square, 2016.

Laplante, Walter. *The Erie Canal* (Road Trip). New York, NY: Gareth Stevens, 2016.

McNeese, Tim. *The Erie Canal: Linking the Great Lakes* (Milestones in American History). New York, NY: Chelsea House Publications, 2009.

Thompson, Linda. *Building the Erie Canal* (History of America). Vero Beach, FL: The Rourke Book Company, 2014.

Winters, Donna, ed. *True Stories of the Erie Canal.* Belen, NM: Bigwater Publishing, 2012.

Wyld, Lionel D. *Low Bridge! Folklore and the Erie Canal.* Syracuse, NY: Syracuse University Press, 2015.

WEBSITES

Because of the changing nature of internet links, Rosen Publishing has developed an online list of websites related to the subject of this book. This site is updated regularly. Please use this link to access this list:

http://www.rosenlinks.com/WEST/Erie

INDEX

L

M

N

O

P

R

S

T

W